This book

Written and compiled by
Sophie Piper
Illustrations copyright © 2008
Mique Moriuchi
This edition copyright © 2008
Lion Hudson

The right of Mique Moriuchi to be
identified as the illustrator of this
work has been asserted by him in
accordance with the Copyright,
Designs and Patents Act 1988.

Published by Lion Children's Books
an imprint of
Lion Hudson plc
Wilkinson House, Jordan Hill Road,
Oxford OX2 8DR, England
www.lionhudson.com/lionchildrens
UK ISBN 978 0 7459 6065 4
US ISBN 978 0 8254 7839 0

First edition 2008

Acknowledgments
All unattributed prayers are by
Sophie Piper and Lois Rock,
copyright © Lion Hudson.
The prayer on page 49 by
Christina Goodings is copyright
© Lion Hudson.

The prayer on page 55 is from
Carmina Gadelica collected by
Alexander Carmichael, published
by Floris Books, Edinburgh.

Bible extracts are taken or adapted
from the Good News Bible,
published by The Bible
Societies/HarperCollins Publishers
Ltd, UK © American Bible Society
1966, 1971, 1976, 1992, used by
permission.

A catalogue record for this book is
available from the British Library

Printed and bound in China, July
2013, LH06

Goodnight
Prayers

Sophie Piper
Mique Moriuchi

LION
CHILDREN'S

The moon shines bright,
The stars give light
Before the break of day;
God bless you all
Both great and small
And send a joyful day.

Traditional

Contents

Night

Day is done,
Gone the sun
From the lake,
From the hills,
From the sky.
Safely rest,
All is well!
God is nigh.

Anonymous

All praise to God for the evening song of the birds. Whatever the day has been like, the birds still carol their cheerful songs as the twilight settles and fades.

Night-time:
the flowers fold their petals
and bow their heads
as if in prayer
to their Maker.

Dear God,
I look around and see all the things you have made: the earth and the sky, the tall mountains and the deep oceans.

You made the sun that rises every morning and you scattered huge handfuls of stars in the night-time sky.

You made all kinds of animals for every place on earth. There on the hills and the plains, in the green fields and the dry deserts, you take care of them all.

You are a great God. I give you all my respect.

From the prayer of Job, in the Bible

Open my eyes, dear God,
To the beauty of the night:
To a world of shape and silhouette,
And scatterings of silver.

I walk with beauty before me.
I walk with beauty behind me.
I walk with beauty above me.
I walk with beauty around me.

Based on a Navajo night chant

The storm may roar,
the wind may blow –
but Love will never
let me go.

The wind may blow,
the storm may roar –
Love keeps me safe
for evermore.

The lightning and thunder
They go and they come;
But the stars and the stillness
Are always at home.

George MacDonald (1824–1905)

An evening prayer
as the sun sinks low:
we thank you, God,
for this world below.

An evening prayer
as the dark comes nigh:
we thank you, God,
for your heaven on high.

Hope

In the quiet night,
I can hear the wind
that blows from heaven,
bringing life and hope
to all the earth.

Dear God,
This is my evening prayer:
Teach me to be careful in what I say.
Keep me from wanting to do wrong.
Keep me safe from every danger.

From Psalm 141, in the Bible

Good people must be wise in what they say. They should speak gently and so avoid quarrels; they should be kind and encouraging, not cruel and name-calling; they should never whisper untrue things about others, but always tell the truth.

From the book of Proverbs, in the Bible

This is what Jesus taught:
'Love the people who don't like you;
pray for those people who are nasty to
you. You are to be good to them just as
God is good to them. For God gives the
sun and rain to bad people as well as
good people.'

From words of Jesus, in the Bible

Love is giving, not taking,
mending, not breaking,
trusting, believing,
never deceiving,
patiently bearing
and faithfully sharing
each joy, every sorrow,
today and tomorrow.

Anonymous

Dear God,
May the people of the world stop fighting.
May they break up their weapons and
   make something useful instead.

May everyone have a safe place to live.
May everyone enjoy the good things of
   your world.

From words of the prophet Micah, in the Bible

May we learn to appreciate different
points of view:
to know that the view from the hill is
    different from the view in the valley;
the view to the east is different from the
    view to the west;
the view in the morning is different from
    the view in the evening;
the view of a parent is different from the
    view of a child;
the view of a friend is different from the
    view of a stranger;
the view of humankind is different from
    the view of God.
May we all learn to see what is good,
what is true, what is worthwhile.

Blessings

Bless the day, dear God,
from sunrise to sunset.

Bless the night, dear God,
from sunset to sunrise.

God bless all those that I love;
God bless all those that love me;
God bless all those that love those that I love,
And all those that love those that love me.

From an old New England sampler

Tucked up in my little bed,
I say a little prayer
For all the people in this house
And people everywhere.

We pray for those for whom today was like the windswept mountain: give them comfort.

We pray for those for whom today was like the stormy sea: give them calm.

We pray for those for whom today was like the darkest night: give them hope.

Deep peace of the running waves to you,
Deep peace of the flowing air to you,
Deep peace of the quiet earth to you,
Deep peace of the shining stars to you,
Deep peace of the shades of night to you,
Moon and stars always giving light to you,
Deep peace of Christ, the Son of Peace,
  to you.

Traditional Gaelic blessing

O God,
as truly as you are our father,
so just as truly you are our mother.
We thank you, God our father,
for your strength and goodness.
We thank you, God our mother,
for the closeness of your caring.
O God, we thank you for the great love
you have for each one of us.

Julian of Norwich

May God bless you and take care of you.
May God be kind to you and do good
things for you.
May God look on you with love and give
you peace.

A blessing from the Bible

A tiny light
A tiny prayer
For God's blessing
Everywhere.

Goodnight

Now I lay me down to sleep,
I pray thee, Lord, thy child to keep;
Thy love to guard me through the night
And wake me in the morning light.

Traditional

Hands together, close your eyes,
Pray to God above
That the night be filled with peace,
And the day with love.

Jesus, tender Shepherd, hear me,
Bless your little lamb tonight;
Through the darkness please be near me;
Keep me safe till morning light.

All this day your hand has led me,
And I thank you for your care;
You have warmed and clothed and fed me;
Listen to my evening prayer.

Mary Lundie Duncan (1814–40)

God has counted the stars in the heavens,
God has counted the leaves on the tree;
God has counted the children on earth:
I know God has counted me.

Clouds in the sky above,
Waves on the sea,
Angels up in heaven
Watching over you and me.

Christina Goodings

Lord, keep us safe this night,
Secure from all our fears;
May angels guard us while we sleep,
Till morning light appears.

John Leland (1754–1841)

From ghoulies and ghosties
Long-leggety beasties
And things that go bump in the night,
Good Lord deliver us.

Traditional Cornish prayer

God loves you, so don't let anything
worry you or frighten you.

Words of an angel, in the Bible

A silver moon
A velvet sky:
May the angels
Watch close by.

A velvet sky
A silver moon:
May I fall asleep
Quite soon.

I see the moon
And the moon sees me;
God bless the moon
And God bless me.

Traditional

Angel of God, my guardian dear
To whom God's love commits me here,
Ever this day be at my side
To light and guard, to rule and guide.

Traditional

Thou angel of God who hast charge
    of me…
Be thou a bright flame before me,
Be thou a guiding star above me,
Be thou a smooth path below me,
And be a kindly shepherd behind me,
Today, tonight, and for ever.

A prayer from the Gaelic tradition

Morning

Dawn is breaking
silver with birdsong
like heaven awakening.

Now is the gentle, joyful morning
Now is the break of day
Now is the time the sun comes shining
Now is the time to pray.

O God,
I will pray to you in the morning,
I will pray to you at sunrise.

I will ask you to show me the way that
I should go.

I will ask you to protect me from the
people who do not like me, who want
to hurt me.

I will trust in you to protect me,
I will trust in your love.

From Psalm 5, in the Bible

Quietly, in the morning,
I rise and look at the sky
To watch the darkness scatter
As sunlight opens the sky.
The day lies clear before me,
All fresh and shining and new,
And then I ask God to guide me
In all that I have to do.

Index of first lines